DISNEY
ZOOTOPIA

Read Along

Read Along

워크북

이 책은 메인북인 **워크북**과 별책인 **스토리북**, 전 2권으로 분리하여 볼 수 있습니다. 스토리북을 통해 영화의 내용을 영어로 가볍게 읽고 워크북으로 알차게 학습해 보세요

---

1 ## 워크북의 구성

스토리북을 네 개의 파트로 나누어 다양한 액티비티를 담았습니다. 워크북에 담긴 즐거운 활동을 통해 영어 실력을 키워 보세요!

Fun Fact

각 파트마다 영화 내용과 관련된 흥미로운 이야기를 수록하여, 스토리북을 보다 알차게 읽을 수 있도록 구성했습니다. 다양한 주제로 쓰여진 흥미로운 글을 통해 영어 읽기의 재미를 느껴 보세요.

Vocabulary

스토리북 본문에서 볼드로 표시된 주요 단어들을 각 파트별로 정리했습니다. 그림과 예문이 함께 나와 있어 단어의 뜻을 쉽게 이해할 수 있습니다.

Learning Activities

다채로운 학습 액티비티로 나만의 영어 실력을 쌓아 보세요. 단어, 표현, 그리고 내용 이해까지 확실하게 짚어 줍니다.

Review

워크북에 수록된 스티커를 이용하여 이야기 지도와 좋아하는 캐릭터에 대한 소개까지 완성해 보세요! 자연스럽게 이야기를 다시 확인하고 정리할 수 있습니다.

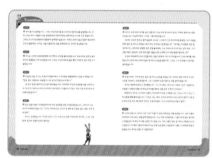

Translation

스토리북의 내용이 완전히 이해되지 않는다면? 워크북 속 친절한 한국어 번역을 확인해 보세요! 최대한 직역에 가깝게 번역되어 원서 읽기의 길잡이가 되어 줍니다.

오디오북

듣기 훈련용   따라 읽기용

QR코드를 인식하여 '듣기 훈련용 오디오북'과 '따라 읽기용 오디오북'의 두 가지 오디오북을 들어 보세요!

'듣기 훈련용 오디오북'은 정식 오디오북으로 오리지널 캐릭터 목소리와 재미있는 효과음이 곁들여져 원서의 내용을 실감나게 듣고 즐길 수 있습니다.

'따라 읽기용 오디오북'은 초보 영어 학습자들을 위해 조금 더 천천히 녹음한 오디오북으로 학습용으로 사용하기에 유용할 것입니다.

2 스토리북의 구성

별책으로 분리하여 더욱 가볍게 읽을 수 있는 스토리북! 간결한 이야기와 함께 영화 속 장면과 대사가 담겨 있어 영화의 재미와 감동을 다시 한 번 느낄 수 있습니다. 이야기에 나오는 주요 단어를 볼드로 강조하여, 문맥 속의 단어들을 더 확실히 인지하도록 도와줍니다.

Contents

· Part ·

1

Amazing teeth

Rabbits' teeth are always growing, and they can grow about 7–12 centimeters each year.

Wild rabbits eat lots of rough foods, like grass, hay, and small tree branches. These foods wear down the teeth.

On the other hand, pet rabbits usually eat softer foods, so they need to chew on special wooden toys to keep their teeth short.

Vocabulary

graduate	졸업하다
academy	학교

bustling	북적거리는

cop	경찰
fellow	동료의
officer	경찰관

department	부서
chief	(조직·집단의) 장(長)

missing	실종된
mammal	포유동물

case	(조사 중인) 사건
assign	(일을) 맡기다, 배정하다

be determined to	~하기로 결심하다	Judy **was determined to** prove that she could be a good cop.
prove	입증하다	
make one's way	나아가다, 가다	Judy saw lots of animals as she **made her way** to her new home.
introduce	소개하다	Judy **introduce**d herself to the other police officers.
priority	우선 사항	The number one **priority** was to find the missing mammals.
parking	주차 (관리)	
duty	직무, 임무	When she found out she had to do **parking** **duty**, Judy was **disappointed**.
disappointed	실망한	
suspicious	수상쩍어하는	Judy was **suspicious** of the fox that went into Jumbeaux's Café.
crush	(희망 등을) 짓밟다	Nick said he did not want to **crush** his son's dreams.
refuse	거절하다	The owner of Jumbeaux's Café **refuse**d to **serve** a Jumbo-pop to Nick.
serve	(음식을) 제공하다	
grumble	투덜거리다	The shop owner **grumble**d and **handed** **over** a Jumbo-pop to Nick.
hand over	건네주다	
treat	특별한 대접	Judy said that the Jumbo-pop was her **treat** for Nick's son.

| **meter maid** | 주차 단속 요원 |
| **ticket** | (교통 위반) 딱지 |

| **goofy** | 엉뚱한 |
| **adorable** | 사랑스러운 |

step in	개입하다
flash	휙 내보이다
badge	(경찰 등의) 신분증

| **melt** | 녹이다 |
| **refreeze** | 다시 얼리다 |

| **cement** | 시멘트 |
| **hop** | 껑충 뛰어들다 |

burn up	분통 터지게 하다	The way other animals treated foxes burned Judy up.
folk	(pl.) 사람들	
backward	뒤떨어진	Judy thought that some folks had backward attitudes about foxes.
attitude	태도, 사고방식	
sidewalk	보도, 인도	Judy saw Nick on the sidewalk later.
turn out	~으로 밝혀지다	It turned out that an adult fox was pretending to be Nick's son.
pair	한 쌍	The pair of foxes fooled Judy because they wanted a free Jumbo-pop.
fool	속이다	
catch up	따라잡다	Judy caught up to Nick on the sidewalk and said that he lied to her.
stand up for	~를 옹호하다	Judy stood up for Nick when he was in Jumbeaux's Café.
shrug	(어깨를) 으쓱하다	Nick shrugged because he did not care what Judy was saying.
hustle	사기 (행위)	Nick used a hustle to get a free Jumbo-pop from Judy.
sly	교활한	Nick thought that he was sly and Judy was dumb.
dumb	멍청한	

Vocabulary Quiz

1 Find hidden words in the puzzle below. Then write down the correct meaning accordingly.

F	Z	T	L	P	R	K	A	F	B	G	A
L	H	D	W	B	A	C	K	W	A	R	D
A	T	B	X	J	I	L	W	F	X	W	O
S	O	U	D	X	R	O	R	D	I	V	R
H	U	S	T	L	E	I	W	H	S	L	A
L	Y	T	W	F	T	A	K	M	L	C	B
B	N	L	G	K	T	M	T	H	Y	Z	L
P	R	I	O	R	I	T	Y	E	N	R	E
A	S	N	S	W	B	S	C	I	G	W	S
H	Q	G	H	F	E	L	L	O	W	A	P
X	Z	T	M	B	J	H	X	Q	H	T	E
E	S	U	S	P	I	C	I	O	U	S	K

fellow	동료의	suspicious		flash	
bustling		sly		backward	
priority		hustle		adorable	

2 Fill in the missing letters for each word. Then complete the answer to the quiz.

1. ma__m__mal 포유동물
2. st___p in 개입하다
3. foo ___ 속이다
4. at___itud___ 태도, 사고방식 *two letters
5. ba___ge (경찰 등의) 신분증
6. ___isapp___inted 실망한 *two letters
7. side___alk 보도, 인도
8. bur___ up 분통 터지게 하다
9. ___reat 특별한 대접
10. h___p 껑충 뛰어들다
11. ___tand up for ~를 옹호하다
12. m___ ___t 녹이다 *two letters
13. fo ___ k (pl.) 사람들

QUIZ

What did the foxes do with the Jumbo-pop that Judy had bought for them?

ANSWER

They m__ __ __ __ __ __ it __ __ __ __

and made "pawpsicles" __ __ __ __ __ __ __ .

Comprehension Quiz

1 Look at the pictures and the description below. Then number them in the correct order to match the story.

Judy made sure Nick's son got a Jumbo-pop.

Judy found out Nick was selling "pawpsicles" to lemmings.

Judy was disappointed because Chief Bogo assigned her parking duty.

Judy moved to Zootopia to become a police officer.

1

2 Choose the best answer for each question.

1 How did Judy feel about moving to Zootopia?

a) Excited about being a cop

b) Nervous about leaving the farm

c) Happy to meet other bunny cops

2 What was Chief Bogo's top priority?

a) Fixing a parking problem

b) Training new police officers

c) Finding the missing mammals

3 What did Judy learn about Nick's son?

a) He stepped into some wet cement.

b) He did not like to eat Jumbo-pops.

c) He was actually another adult fox.

3 Read each sentence and decide whether it is true or false.

1 Zootopia had never had a bunny cop before.	true	false
2 A few officers were assigned to parking duty with Judy.	true	false
3 The owner of Jumbeaux's Café did not want to sell a Jumbo-pop to Nick.	true	false
4 Nick used the Jumbo-pop to make the "pawpsicles."	true	false
5 Judy still felt good about Nick even after she saw him sell "pawpsicles."	true	false

• Part •

2

From the tree tops to the tree bottoms

Sloths spend most of their time in the trees, but what happens when they fall off a branch?

Don't worry—sloths can fall more than 100 feet (30.48 meters) without getting hurt. Their bodies are specially designed so that they can survive a fall. That's good news because they fall about once a week on average.

Vocabulary

weasel [동물] 족제비
chase 뒤쫓다
bandit 강도

upset 속상한

deputy 부관, 대리의
mayor 시장
thrilled 아주 흥분한

clue 단서

sloth [동물] 나무늘보

parking lot 주차장

damage	손상, 피해	There was a lot of damage from Judy's chase with the weasel.
confused	혼란스러워하는	Judy was confused about why Chief Bogo was angry.
chance	기회	Judy got a chance to be a real cop by looking for Mr. Otterton.
strike out	실패하다	Judy could not strike out, or else she would have to resign.
resign	(일에서) 물러나다	
gulp	(두려움에) 침을 꿀꺽 삼키다	Judy gulped when she made a deal with Chief Bogo to find Mr. Otterton.
deal	합의, 거래	
commit	(범죄를) 저지르다	Nick accidentally told Judy that he had committed a crime.
crime	범죄	
approach	접촉하다	Judy approached Flash the sloth and asked him to run a license plate number.
run	처리하다	
stall	시간을 끌다	Nick stalled Judy on purpose because he wanted her to give up.
give up	포기하다	

Vocabulary

rip 찢다, 떼어 내다
shred 조각

jaguar [동물] 재규어
bruised 멍든

lunge 달려들다

demand 요구하다

step forward 도와주려고 나서다

traffic 교통

grab 붙잡다

be about to	막 ~하려고 하다	Judy was not about to drop Mr. Otterton's case.
drop	그만두다	
track	추적하다	Judy and Nick tracked a limo with the license plate number.
attack	공격하다	Mr. Manchas said that Mr. Otterton attacked him in the limo.
teensy	아주 작은	Nick and Judy were surprised that a teensy otter could hurt Mr. Manchas.
otter	[동물] 수달	
mumble	중얼거리다	Mr. Otterton was mumbling in the limo about "night howlers."
savage	몹시 사나운	Mr. Otterton went savage and attacked Mr. Manchas.
capture	붙잡다	Judy and Nick tried to capture Mr. Manchas, but failed.
technically	엄밀히 따지면	Nick told Chief Bogo that Judy technically still had time to finish the case.
lead	실마리	Nick and Judy followed the lead to try to crack the case.
crack	해결하다	
bet	장담하다	Nick bet that the "night howlers" had took Mr. Otterton.

1 Use the clues below to fill in the crossword puzzle.

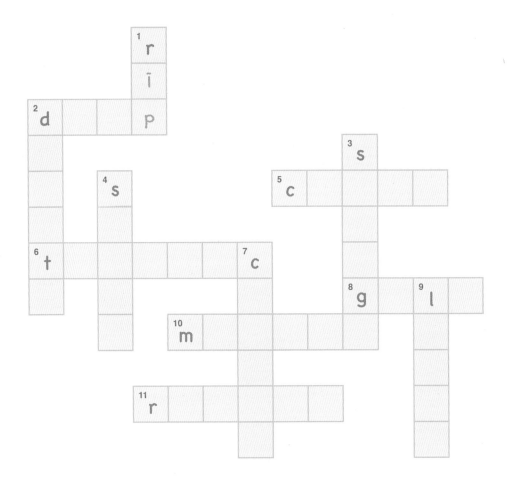

★ ACROSS ★		★ DOWN ★	
2 그만두다	**5** 해결하다	**1** 찢다, 떼어 내다	**2** 부관, 대리의
6 교통	**8** 침을 꿀꺽 삼키다	**3** 몹시 사나운	**4** 시간을 끌다
10 중얼거리다	**11** (일에서) 물러나다	**7** (범죄를) 저지르다	**9** 달려들다

2 Fill in the missing letters for each word. Then complete the answer to the quiz.

① __eensy 아주 작은

② bru__sed 멍든

③ da__ag__ 손상, 피해 *two letters

④ c__u__ 단서 *two letters

⑤ con__used 혼란스러워하는

⑥ be__ 장담하다

⑦ __trike __ut 실패하다 *two letters

⑧ __ead 실마리

⑨ gi__e up 포기하다

⑩ d__al 합의, 거래

⑪ te__hnically 엄밀히 따지면

⑫ tr__ck 추적하다

⑬ __hred 조각

⑭ ott__r [동물] 수달

QUIZ

What did Nick say to defend Judy from Chief Bogo?

ANSWER

That Judy still had __ __ __ __ __ __ __ __ __ __

to __ __ __ __ __ __ the __ __ __ __ __

1 **Choose the sentence which best describes the picture to match the story.**

Ⓐ Mr. Manchas got angry because Judy and Nick looked inside his limo.

Ⓑ Mr. Manchas started to howl at Judy and Nick.

Ⓒ Mr. Manchas became savage and tried to attack Judy and Nick.

Ⓐ Deputy Mayor Bellwether showed pictures of Mr. Otterton.

Ⓑ Deputy Mayor Bellwether showed Nick and Judy her traffic cameras.

Ⓒ Deputy Mayor Bellwether asked Nick and Judy for their help.

2 Choose the best answer for each question.

1 Why did the pig ask for Judy's help?

    a) A weasel robbed his shop.

    b) A weasel broke all his flowers.

    c) A weasel damaged Little Rodentia.

2 What was Mr. Otterton doing in the photo that Judy saw?

    a) Talking to Nick

    b) Eating a pawpsicle

    c) Getting into a car

3 What did Chief Bogo do when he found out Mr. Manchas had escaped?

    a) He asked Nick to help with the case.

    b) He told Judy to give him her badge.

    c) He started to look for Mr. Manchas himself.

3 Read each sentence and decide whether it is true or false.

1 Deputy Mayor Bellwether was happy that Judy was taking the Otterton case.	true	false
2 Nick knew that Flash would work very slowly.	true	false
3 Nick was surprised that an otter could hurt Mr. Manchas.	true	false
4 Nick asked Chief Bogo for an extra forty-eight hours to look for Mr. Otterton.	true	false
5 It was Judy's idea to look at the traffic cameras to find Mr. Manchas.	true	false

🔊 **Listen and read the characters' words.**

Listen to the "Listen & Read Along" audio file and repeat after each sentence, focusing on your pause (**/**), stress (**bold**), and linking (⌒).

Hey. / Officer Hopps. / You **ready** to make the world a better place?

And finally, / our first bunny, / Officer Hopps. / **Parking** duty.

My boy, / this **goofy little** stinker, he loves all things elephant. / Wants to be **one** when he grows up.

• Part •

3

I see you!

A sheep's pupil, the small black area in the center of the eye, is shaped like a rectangle instead of a circle. This means the sheep can see almost everything around it except for things right behind it.

Predators such as coyotes, dogs, and mountain lions try to hunt sheep. So, sheep need to keep an eye on their surroundings.

entrance 입구, 문
guard 지키다

howl (개 등이) 길게 울다
distracted 산만해진
sneak 살금살금 가다
(과거형 snuck)

row 열, 줄
cage 우리

imprisoned 감금된
predator 포식 동물
include 포함하다

record 녹화하다

figure out	알아내다	Nick **figured out** where the night howlers went.
asylum	정신 병원	Judy and Nick went to the Cliffside **Asylum** to look for Mr. Otterton.
impressed	감명을 받은	Judy was **impressed** because Nick knew where the night howlers were.
junior	하위의, 부하의	Judy thought that Nick would be a good **junior** detective.
detective	형사, 수사관	
hand out	나눠 주다	Judy saw all the missing mammals that were on the files Chief Bogo had **handed out**.
footstep	발소리	Nick and Judy hid when they heard some **footsteps**.
narrowly	가까스로	Nick and Judy **narrowly** escaped getting caught by the mayor.
escape	탈출하다	
present	제시하다	Judy made a recording of the mayor and **presented** it to Chief Bogo.
arrest	체포하다	Chief Bogo said that Judy could **arrest** the mayor.
appointed	임명된	A new mayor of Zootopia was **appointed**.

Vocabulary

press conference
기자 회견

storm off (화를 내며) 뛰쳐나가다

divide 분열시키다

chaos 혼돈, 혼란

edge 끝, 가장자리
crop (농)작물

family	(동물) 과(科)	The missing mammals were all part of the predator **family**.
survive	생존하다	Predators had to hunt and fight to **survive**.
aggressive **instinct**	공격적인 본능	Predators had to use their **aggressive instinct**s for their survival.
revert	되돌아가다	Judy said that predators were **revert**ing to their old ways.
primitive	원시적인	Predators had started doing their **primitive** habits again.
prey	먹이	**Prey** and predators had different opinions about the press conference.
overhear	우연히 듣다 (과거형 overheard)	Judy **overheard** her father talking to some kids.
scold	야단치다	Judy's father **scold**ed some kids at the edge of his field.
refer	(~라고) 부르다	Gideon **refer**red to the flowers in the field as night howlers.
go crazy	정신이 이상해지다	Judy learned that the night howler flowers made some animals **go crazy**.

Vocabulary Quiz

1 Find hidden words in the puzzle below. Then write down the correct meaning accordingly.

R	E	V	E	R	T	C	P	B	C	S	F
T	L	H	K	I	Q	H	G	M	H	B	A
J	D	N	F	Y	V	E	U	E	A	L	Z
M	O	A	O	T	F	J	A	X	O	W	R
D	V	U	O	N	A	R	R	E	S	T	T
J	E	M	T	N	X	T	D	A	C	N	K
F	R	Q	S	H	I	F	O	Z	M	J	P
A	H	F	T	J	B	L	S	N	E	A	K
F	E	Z	E	C	M	V	L	S	R	M	W
S	A	P	P	O	I	N	T	E	D	W	X
H	R	T	S	A	E	H	M	P	A	S	C
S	O	Q	I	N	S	T	I	N	C	T	V

footstep

appointed

chaos

guard

revert

sneak

instinct

overhear

arrest

2 Fill in the missing letters for each word. Then complete the answer to the quiz.

① ___owl (개 등이) 길게 울다   ② incl__de 포함하다

③ p__imi__ive 원시적인 *two letters   ④ __rop (농)작물

⑤ st__r__ off (화를 내며) 뛰쳐나가다 *two letters

⑥ i__pressed 감명을 받은

⑦ __ntra__ce 입구, 문 *two letters   ⑧ de__ective 형사, 수사관

⑨ __cold 야단치다   ⑩ __rey 먹이

⑪ imp__ison__d 감금된 *two letters

⑫ __istr__c__ed 산만해진 *three letters   ⑬ r__w 열, 줄

⑭ p__e__ent 제시하다 *two letters

QUIZ

How did Nick feel at the press conference?

ANSWER

Nick was deeply __ __ __ __ by Judy's __ __ __ __ __ __ __ __ __

about __ __ __ __ __ __ __ __ .

1 **Look at the pictures and the description below. Then number them in the correct order to match the story.**

Judy realized the night howlers were flowers making the predators turn savage.

Nick and Judy recorded the mayor with a phone.

Nick and Judy found the predators in cages.

Judy explained about the predators at the press conference.

2 Choose the best answer for each question.

1 Who figured out that the wolves were going to the Cliffside Asylum?

 a) Judy

 b) Nick

 c) Bellwether

2 Why did Nick and Judy almost get caught when they were recording the mayor?

 a) Their footsteps were too loud.

 b) Nick started laughing.

 c) Judy's phone started ringing.

3 Why did Judy's father scold some kids?

 a) They were running through some flowers.

 b) They were picking his flowers.

 c) They were digging up the field.

3 Read each sentence and decide whether it is true or false.

1 Judy distracted the wolves at the Cliffside Asylum by giving them some food.   true   false

2 The mayor already knew about the savage animals in cages.   true   false

3 Chief Bogo told Judy that she could arrest the mayor.   true   false

4 Nick was mad at Judy because she did not invite him to the press conference.   true   false

5 The animals in Zootopia agreed about what Judy said at the press conference.   true   false

· Part ·

4

The city life of foxes

Urban foxes—that is, foxes that live in cities—are common sights in Europe, the U.S., Canada, and Australia. They eat everything from worms, insects, and birds to human foods such as cheese and bread.

Some people love having these interesting visitors to their yard. Others think they are a pest, especially since their screams are noisy and can sound like a person!

Vocabulary

lab 실험실

abandoned 버려진

ram [동물] 숫양

poison 독
pellet 작은 알약

apologize	사과하다	Judy **apologize**d to Nick for saying bad things about predators.
ignorant **irresponsible**	무지한 무책임한	Judy thought that her comments about predators were **ignorant** and **irresponsible**.
small-minded	속이 좁은	Judy did not want to be **small-minded** about predators anymore.
sincere	진심의	Nick thought that Judy was being **sincere** when she apologized.
forgive	용서하다 (과거형 forgave)	Nick **forgave** Judy for what she did.
shoot	(총 등을) 쏘다	The rams could **shoot** the pellets at predators.
evidence	증거	The poison pellets could be **evidence** to prove what really had happened.
collide	충돌하다	The subway car almost **collide**d with another train.
in charge	~을 책임지는	Mayor Bellwether wanted prey to be **in charge** of Zootopia.

take control of
~을 제어하다

derail   탈선하다
catch on fire   불붙다
destroy   파괴하다

race   급히 가다
dash   급히 달려가다

smirk   능글맞게 웃다

knock	치다	The rams knocked the case of evidence out of Nick's hands.
dart	(화살 등을) 쏘다	Mayor Bellwether wanted to dart every predator in Zootopia to keep her power.
swap	바꾸다	Nick had swapped the poison pellet with a blueberry.
trick	속이다	Nick tricked Mayor Bellwether into confessing what she did.
confess	고백하다	
against	~에 반대하여	Mayor Bellwether said that it was her story against Nick and Judy's.
return	돌아오다	Life in Zootopia returned to normal after Mayor Bellwether was arrested.
remind	상기시키다	Judy reminded the new police officers that they could make things better.
proudly	자랑스럽게	Judy proudly smiled at Nick when he graduated from the police academy.
resident	주민, 거주자	The residents of Zootopia could make their home better if they worked together.

Vocabulary Quiz

1 Use the clues below to fill in the crossword puzzle.

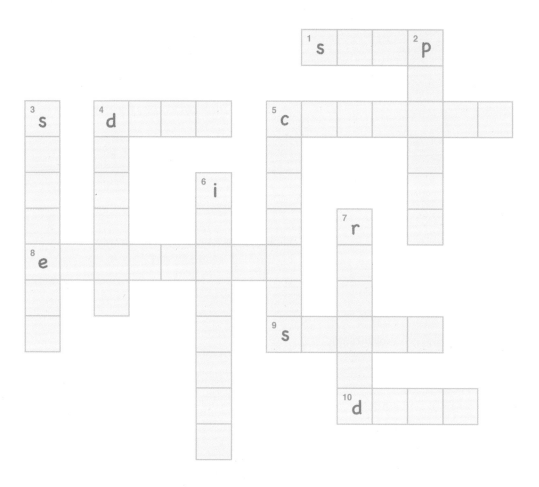

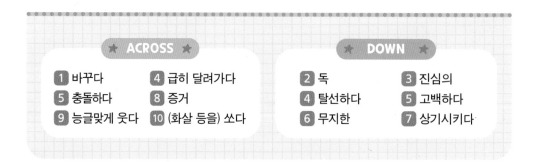

★ ACROSS ★

1 바꾸다
4 급히 달려가다
5 충돌하다
8 증거
9 능글맞게 웃다
10 (화살 등을) 쏘다

★ DOWN ★

2 독
3 진심의
4 탈선하다
5 고백하다
6 무지한
7 상기시키다

2 Fill in the missing letters for each word. Then complete the answer to the quiz.

① __mall-minded 속이 좁은   ② in c__arge ~을 책임지는

③ kn__ck 치다   ④ __rick 속이다

⑤ la__ 실험실   ⑥ pe__let 작은 알약

⑦ ret__rn 돌아오다   ⑧ rac__ 급히 가다

⑨ a__andon__d 버려진 *two letters

⑩ i__ __esponsible 무책임한 *two letters

⑪ proudl__ 자랑스럽게

QUIZ

Why did Nick NOT turn savage after being shot?

ANSWER

Bellwether ___ ___ ___ ___ him with a

___ ___ ___ ___ ___ ___ ___ .

Comprehension **Quiz**

1 **Choose the sentence which best describes the picture to match the story.**

A Rams were creating medicine to fix the savage animals.

B Rams were making poison pellets to make predators go savage.

C Rams were using guns to protect themselves from savage predators.

A Nick and Judy followed Bellwether to the Cliffside Asylum.

B Nick and Judy secretly recorded Bellwether's confession.

C Nick and Judy convinced Bellwether to set the caged animals free.

2 Choose the best answer for each question.

1 How did Judy get back to Zootopia?

a) By getting a ride from Nick

b) By taking the subway

c) By driving a blueberry truck

2 What kind of evidence were Nick and Judy taking to the ZPD in the case?

a) A gun and a poison pellet

b) Some night howler flowers

c) Pictures of the secret lab

3 What did Nick do after graduating from the police academy?

a) He looked for the lost mammals.

b) He had parking duty.

c) He became Judy's partner.

3 Read each sentence and decide whether it is true or false.

❶ Nick did not believe Judy's apology.	true	false
❷ Bellwether wanted prey to rule Zootopia.	true	false
❸ Nick was only pretending to turn savage.	true	false
❹ Judy and Nick swapped a poison pellet with a blueberry.	true	false
❺ Nick gave a speech at the police academy graduation.	true	false

📣 Listen and read the characters' words.

Listen to the "Listen & Read Along" audio file and repeat after each sentence, focusing on your pause (/), stress (**bold**), and linking (⌢).

You know, I think you'd **actually** make a pretty good **cop**.

For whatever reason, / they seem to be reverting **back** to their primitive savage ways.

The **flowers** are making the predators go savage. / That's **it**! / **That's** what I've been missing!

I have to fix this, / but I can't do it without **you**.

Fear **always** works. / And I'll **dart** every predator in Zootopia to **keep** it that way.

It's my word **against** yours!

It's called a **hustle**, / sweetheart.

Story Map

Follow the story line and put the stickers on their correct places!

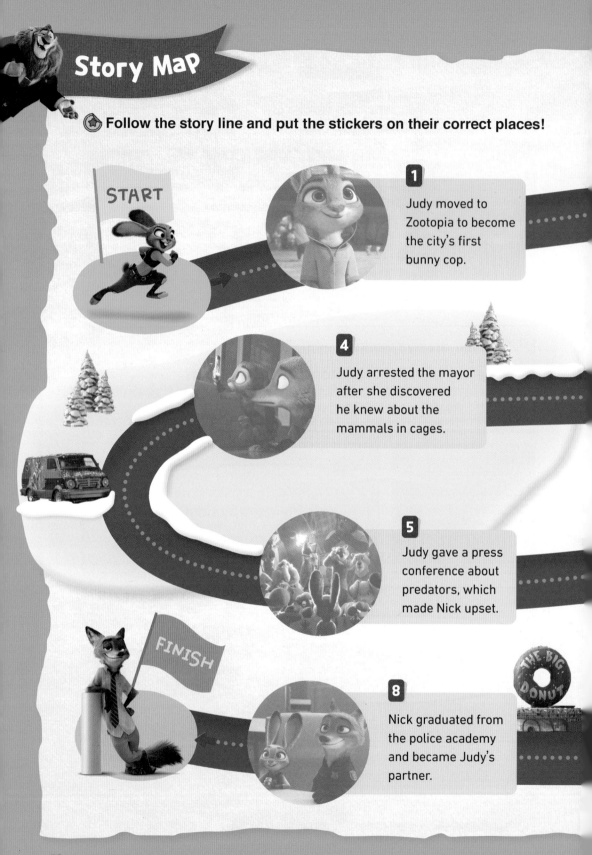

START

1
Judy moved to Zootopia to become the city's first bunny cop.

4
Judy arrested the mayor after she discovered he knew about the mammals in cages.

5
Judy gave a press conference about predators, which made Nick upset.

FINISH

THE BIG DONUT

8
Nick graduated from the police academy and became Judy's partner.

2 Nick hustled Judy but later helped her look for Mr. Otterton.

3 Nick and Judy found the missing mammals at the Cliffside Asylum.

6 Judy and Nick found out the rams were making poison pellets to make the predators turn savage.

7 Nick and Judy tricked Bellwether and recorded her confessing to making the predators turn savage.

Character Chart

✏️ **Choose your favorite character and describe them using the words from the personality bank.**

Personality Bank

cunning 교활한 | optimistic 낙관적인 | dishonest 정직하지 못한

resourceful 재치있는 | easy-going 태평한 | reliable 믿음직한

ruthless 인정사정없는 | determined 단호한 | realistic 현실적인

polite 예의 바른 | sociable 사교적인 | street-smart 세상 물정에 밝은

Stick Here!

My favorite character is

_____ .

I think _____ is

_____ ,

_____ , and

_____ .

* There is an example answer for you to refer to on page 67.

ZOOTOPIA

Read Along

Translation

p.2

주디 홉스는 들떴습니다. 그녀는 자신의 동기들 중 수석으로 경찰 학교를 졸업했습니다. 이제 그녀는 자기 가족들이 사는 농장을 떠나 주토피아라는 북적거리는 도시로 가고 있었습니다. 그녀는 도시의 첫 번째 토끼 경찰관이 될 예정이었습니다. 아무도 토끼가 좋은 경찰이 될 것이라고 믿지 않았지만, 주디는 그들이 틀렸다는 것을 증명하겠다고 단단히 결심했습니다!

p.3

주디는 그녀의 아파트를 향해 나아가면서, 주변을 둘러보았습니다. 주토피아는 온갖 모습과 크기의 동물들로 가득 차 있었습니다! 그녀는 자신의 새로운 삶을 빨리 시작하고 싶어 견딜 수가 없었습니다!

p.4

다음 날 아침, 주디는 주토피아 경찰서에서 그녀의 동료 경찰들에게 자신을 소개했습니다. "안녕. 홉스 경관이야. 세상을 더 나은 곳으로 만들 준비가 됐니?"

곧 보고 경찰서장이 안으로 걸어 들어왔습니다. "우리에게 14건의 포유동물 실종 사건이 있다. 14건이나 말이야! 우리가 이제까지 겪어 왔던 사건들보다 더 많지. 이게 가장 우선적으로 처리해야 될 일이야."

p.5

보고 경찰서장은 각 경찰관마다 한 건의 포유동물 실종 사건을 맡겼습니다. 그러다가 그는 주디의 차례까지 왔습니다. "그리고 마지막으로, 우리의 첫 번째 토끼 경찰, 홉스 경관. 주차 단속 임무."

주디는 실망했습니다. 하지만 만약 그녀가 주차 단속 요원이 되어야만 한다면, 그녀는 가능한 한 최고의 요원이 되려고 했어요!

🌑 주디가 주차 위반 딱지를 끊고 있을 때 그녀는 여우 한 마리가 점보즈 카페로 들어가는 것을 보았습니다. 미심쩍어하며, 그녀는 그를 따라갔습니다.

하지만 그녀가 안으로 들어섰을 때, 주디는 그 여우가 그저 코끼리처럼 분장한, 자기 아들을 위해 점보-팝 아이스크림을 사려고 하는 것이라는 걸 알았습니다. "내 아들, 이 엉뚱한 작은 말썽꾸러기는, 코끼리와 관련된 모든 것을 좋아해요. 그는 자라서 코끼리가 되고 싶어 하죠. 그거 정말 귀엽지 않아요? 그의 작은 꿈을 짓밟는다면 도대체 내가 어떤 동물이겠어요, 네?"

주인이 여우에게 아이스크림을 파는 것을 거부하자, 주디가 끼어들어서 그녀의 배지를 내보였습니다. 만약 어린 여우가 점보-팝 아이스크림을 원한다면, 그녀는 그가 꼭 얻을 수 있게 할 셈이었습니다!

🌑 투덜거리며, 가게 주인은 점보-팝 아이스크림을 건넸습니다. 하지만 아빠 여우가 자신의 지갑을 꺼내려고 손을 뻗었을 때, 그는 자신에게 지갑이 없다는 것을 알아차렸습니다.

주디는 계산해 주겠다고 제안했습니다. "오, 아니에요, 제가 사는 거예요. 단지—알잖아요, 사람들이 저렇게 뒤떨어진 태도로 여우를 대하는 것을 보면 전 화가 나거든요."

바깥에서, 주디는 닉이라는 이름의, 여우에게 자신을 소개했습니다. 그러고 나서 그녀는 그의 아들을 향해 돌아섰습니다. "그리고 너는, 얘야. 넌 커서 코끼리가 되고 싶다고 했지? 그럼 넌 코끼리가 될 거야, 왜냐하면 여기는 주토피아잖아. 누구나 무엇이든지 될 수 있어."

🌑 시간이 흐른 뒤, 주디는 닉과 그의 "아들"이 보도 위에 있는 것을 보았습니다. 닉의 아들이 어린아이가 아니라는 것을 알게 되었습니다. 그는 어른 여우였어요! 그 둘은 무료 점보-팝 아이스크림을 얻기 위해서 주디를 속였던 것이었습니다. 이제 그들은 점보-팝 아이스크림을 녹이고 그것을 다시 더 작은 "발바닥 막대 아이스크림"으로 얼리고 있었으며, 이를 나그네쥐에게 팔고 있었습니다. 주디는 믿을 수가 없었어요!

p.9

● 주디는 닉을 따라잡았습니다. "내가 네 편을 들어줬잖아, 그런데 넌 나에게 거짓말을 했어!"

닉은 어깨를 으쓱거렸습니다. "그게 바로 사기라는 거야, 얘야. 좋아, 봐, 모두가 그들이 원하는 대로 무엇이든지 될 수 있다고 믿으면서 주토피아로 오지. 글쎄, 넌 그럴 수 없어. 넌 단지 네 원래의 모습만이 될 수 있을 뿐이야."

닉이 자신을 가리켰습니다—"교활한 여우"—그다음에는 주디를 가리켰습니다—"멍청한 토끼."

그 말은 주디의 마음을 상하게 했습니다. "나는 멍청한 토끼가 *아니야!*"

"그래. 그럼 저건 마르지 않은 시멘트가 아니겠지."

주디는 아래를 내려다보았습니다. 그녀는 말라가는 시멘트 속으로 뛰어들었던 것입니다.

닉이 자신의 고개를 저었습니다. "넌 절대로 진정한 경찰이 될 수 없어."

p.10

● 다음 날, 어떤 돼지가 주디에게 달려왔습니다. 그의 꽃가게가 방금 족제비에게 도둑맞았기 때문이었어요!

주디는 그 강도를 쫓아서 리틀 로덴시아의 곳곳을 누비다가 마침내 그를 붙잡았습니다. 하지만 주디가 그 도둑을 ZPD(주토피아 경찰서)로 데려왔을 때, 보고 서장은 화를 냈습니다. 그 추격이 큰 피해를 일으켰던 것입니다.

주디는 혼란스러워했습니다. "서장님, 전 나쁜 녀석을 잡았어요. 그게 바로 제 일이고요."

"네 일은 주차된 차들에 딱지를 끊는 거야."

◉ 갑자기, 주디와 보고 서장의 대화는 매우 속상해하는 오터튼 부인에 의해 중단되었습니다. 그녀의 남편은 열흘 동안이나 실종된 상태였습니다!

주디는 이게 바로 그녀의 기회라는 것을 알았습니다. 그녀는 오터튼 씨를 찾겠다고 나섰습니다.

보고 서장이 뭐라고 하기 전에, 벨웨더 부시장이 나타났습니다. 그녀는 주디가 그 사건을 맡으려고 한다는 이야기를 들었습니다. 그녀는 정말 기뻐했습니다.

보고 서장은 다른 방법이 없었습니다. "난 너에게 48시간을 주겠어. 하지만, 네가 실패하면, 사직하는 거야."

주디는 침을 꿀꺽 삼켰습니다. "오, 어. . . 좋아요. 그렇게 하죠."

◉ 이 사건에서 주디가 가진 유일한 단서는 오터튼 씨의 사진이었습니다. 사진 속에서, 그는 발바닥 막대 아이스크림을 먹고 있었어요. 그건 바로 닉이 그를 알고 있다는 것을 의미했죠!

주디는 그 교활한 여우를 찾아 나섰습니다. 그녀는 그가 범죄를 저질렀다는 사실을 인정하도록 그를 속였고 그가 그녀를 돕는 것을 승낙하게 했습니다.

◉ 주디와 닉은 곧 오터튼 씨가 29THD03이라고 쓰여진 자동차 번호판을 단 차량에 오르는 모습이 목격되었다는 것을 알아냈습니다. 두 동물은 DMV(교통국)로 갔는데, 그곳에서는 닉의 친구인 나무늘보 플래시가 일했습니다.

주디는 플래시에게 다가갔습니다. "음, 전 당신이 우리를 위해 차량 번호를 검색해 주었으면 해요."

플래시는 승낙했습니다. 하지만 그 나무늘보가 너무 천천히 움직여서 주디에게 답을 주기까지 하루 종일 걸렸습니다! 닉은 플래시와 말하는 것이 주디를 지연시키게 될 것을 알고 있었습니다. 그는 그녀를 포기하게 만들려고 노력하고 있었어요! 하지만 토끼는 사건을 포기하려 들지 않았습니다.

p.14

● 마침내, 닉과 주디는 오터튼 씨가 리무진의 뒷좌석에 탄 채로 떠났다는 것을 알게 되었습니다. 그 두 친구는 어떤 주차장까지 그 리무진을 추적해 갔습니다. 그들이 그 안을 들여다보았을 때, 그들은 충격을 받았습니다. 뒷좌석이 갈기갈기 찢겨 있었습니다.

그 둘은 운전자인, 만차스 씨라는 이름의 재규어를 찾아 나섰습니다. 만차스 씨가 그의 집 문을 열었을 때, 두 동물은 그가 맞아서 몹시 멍이 든 것을 보았습니다. 그는 그들에게 오터튼 씨가 자신을 공격했다고 말했어요!

p.15

● "우와. 그 자그마한 수달이. . .그런 짓을 했다고요?"

만차스 씨는 오터튼 씨가 "나이트 하울러(night howlers)"에 대해서 중얼거리다가 야만적으로 변했다고 설명했습니다.

갑자기, 만차스 씨가 네 발로 엎드렸습니다. 경고도 없이, 그는 닉과 주디에게 달려들었습니다. 그도 역시, 야만적으로 변해 버렸어요!

p.16

● 닉과 주디는 만차스 씨를 붙잡으려고 했지만, 그는 도망치고 말았습니다. 그들이 보고 서장에게 무슨 일이 일어났는지 설명하자, 그는 주디의 배지를 달라고 요구했습니다.

주디가 응하기 전에, 닉이 나섰습니다. "문제가 있어요, 서장님, 당신은 그녀에게 48시간을 주었잖아요, 그래서 엄밀히 말하자면 우리에게는 오터튼 씨를 찾는 데 아직 10시간이 남아 있는 거예요. 그리고 그게 정확히 우리가 지금 하려고 하는 일이죠. 그러니까 당신이 우리를 양해해 준다면, 우리에게는 따라가야 할 아주 중요한 실마리와 해결해야 할 사건이 있어요."

닉이 그녀의 편을 들어준 것을 보고 주디는 놀랐습니다. 그녀가 처음에 생각했던 것보다 그 여우에게 좋은 면이 더 있다는 것을 그녀는 깨달았습니다. 어쩌면 그 둘은 결국 그렇게 다르지 않을지도 모르죠.

p.17

● 그때 닉에게 좋은 생각이 떠올랐습니다. 그들이 교통 카메라를 이용해서 그 야만스럽게 변한 만차스 씨가 어디로 가 버렸는지 확인할 수 있다는 것이었죠.

닉과 주디는 벨웨더 부시장을 찾아갔습니다. 그 둘은 그녀의 카메라를 통해서 한 무리의 늑대들이 승합차에서 뛰어나와서 만차스 씨를 붙잡는 것을 보았습니다.

늑대들 중 하나가 울부짖자, 주디는 무언가를 깨달았습니다. "나이트 하울러. 저게 바로 만차스가 두려워한 거였어…늑대들 말이야! 늑대들이 밤에 짖는 동물들(나이트 하울러)이잖아. 만약 그들이 만차스를 데려갔다면…"

"그들은 또한, 오터튼도 데려간 게 틀림없어."

p.18

● 닉은 화면을 살펴보았습니다. 늑대들이 어디로 가고 있는지를 그가 알아내는 데는 그리 오래 걸리지 않았습니다: 바로 클리프사이드 정신 병원이었습니다.

주디는 감명을 받았습니다. "자 너 좀 봐, 예비 경찰관 같아. 있잖아, 내 생각에 넌 꽤 괜찮은 경찰이 될 것 같아."

그 둘이 정신 병원에 다다랐을 때, 그들은 늑대들이 입구를 지키고 있다는 것을 알게 되었습니다. 주디가 길게 울었어요. 곧 모든 늑대들도 마찬가지로, 울부짖었습니다.

p.19

● 늑대들의 정신이 산만해진 사이에, 주디와 닉은 안으로 몰래 들어갔고…그곳에서 그들은 감금된 포식 동물들이 들어 있는 우리들이 줄 지어 서 있는 것을 발견했습니다—오터튼 씨를 포함해서 말이에요!

주디는 우리의 수를 셌습니다: "…열하나, 열둘, 열셋, 열넷. 보고 서장님이 열네 건의 포유동물 실종 사건 파일을 나눠 주었어. 실종된 모든 포유동물들이 바로 여기에 있어."

p.20

● 갑자기, 닉과 주디는 발소리를 들었습니다. 그 둘은 숨었습니다. 잠시 뒤, 그들은 어떤 목소리를 들었습니다. 그건 바로 시장의 목소리였어요. 그는 야만적으로 변한 동물들에 대해 다 알고 있었고 그것을 비밀로 하고 있었습니다!

자신의 전화를 꺼내서, 주디는 시장을 촬영했습니다. 그때 그녀의 전화가 울리기 시작했어요. 그들이 잡히기 전에 그녀와 닉은 정신 병원에서 탈출해야만 했습니다!

p.22

● 두 사람은 가까스로 탈출했습니다. 다시 ZPD로 돌아와서, 주디는 그녀가 촬영한 것을 보고 서장에게 제출했습니다. 감명을 받고는, 그는 *그녀가* 시장을 체포할 수 있게 해 주었습니다.

잠시 뒤에, 새로 임명된 벨웨더 시장은 기자 회견을 열었습니다. 주디가 질문에 답을 하게 되었을 때, 그녀는 야만스럽게 변한 동물들에 대한 사실들을 이야기했습니다.

p.23

● "우리가 아는 것이라고는 그들이 모두 포식 동물과(科)에 속한다는 것입니다. 수천 년 전에, 포식 동물들은 그들의 공격적인 사냥 본능을 통해 생존했습니다. 어떤 이유에서인지, 그들은 다시 자신들의 원시적이고 야만적인 방식으로 되돌아가고 있는 것 같습니다."

그녀의 말에 닉은 상처받았습니다. 그가 야만적인 포식 동물로 변할 수 있다고 그녀는 생각했던 것일까요?

주디에게서 돌아서면서, 닉은 자리를 박차고 떠났습니다.

p.24

● 기자 회견은 주토피아를 분열시켰습니다. 곧 먹이와 포식자 간의 싸움이 되었습니다.

주디는 자신이 초래한 혼란에 대해 몹시 죄책감을 느껴서 그녀는 ZPD를 그만두고 집에 왔습니다. 며칠 뒤, 그녀는 그녀의 아버지가 자기 밭 가장자리에 있는 꽃 사이로 뛰어다닌 것을 두고 몇몇 아이들을 야단치는 것을 우연히 들었습니다.

p.25

● 주디가 자기 아버지의 친구인 기디온이 같은 꽃을 두고 나이트 하울러라고 부르는 것을 들었을 때, 그녀는 무언가를 깨달았습니다. "나이트 하울러는 늑대가 아니었어. 그것들은 꽃이었어."

주디의 아버지는 그 꽃들이 그의 작물들에서 벌레를 쫓지만, 그것들은 또한 동물들을 미치게 만들기도 한다고 설명했습니다.

주디는 오터튼 씨가 꽃집 주인이라는 사실이 그녀의 사건 파일에 있던 것을 기억했습니다. "꽃들이 포식자들을 야만적으로 변하게 한 거야. 바로 그거야! 그게 바로 내가 놓치고 있던 부분이었어!"

p.26

● 주디는 그들의 가족이 사용하는 블루베리 트럭에 급히 올라탔고 도시로 다시 달려갔습니다. 그녀는 닉을 찾아서 그에게 사과했습니다. "나는 무지했고 무책임했고 옹졸했어. 나는 이 일을 해결해야만 해, 하지만 난 너 없이는 그렇게 할 수 없어."

닉은 주디가 진심이라는 것을 알았습니다. 그는 그녀를 용서해 주었습니다.

p.27

● 주디는 닉에게 그녀가 꽃에 대해 무엇을 알아냈는지를 말해 주었습니다. 함께, 그들은 자신들의 단서를 따라서 버려진 지하철 차량 안에 있는 비밀 실험실로 향했습니다. 안에서, 한 무리의 숫양들이 나이트 하울러를 포식자들에게 쏘면 그들을 야만적으로 변하게 할 독이 든 작은 탄알로 바꾸고 있었습니다.

주디는 그들이 무엇을 해야만 하는지 알았습니다. "우리는 이 증거를 ZPD로 가져가야 해!"

p.28

🔵 닉과 주디는 지하철 차량을 빼앗았습니다. 하지만 숫양들이 그들을 막으려고 했습니다. 다른 기차와 충돌할 뻔한 후에, 그들의 기차는 탈선했고 불이 붙으면서, 꽃들을 소실시켰습니다. 닉은 총과 나이트 하울러 탄알이 안에 들어 있는 보관함을 들어 올렸습니다. 그들에게는 여전히 그들의 증거가 있었습니다!

두 동물은 ZPD로 가기 위해 자연사 박물관 사이를 빠르게 달려갔습니다. 갑자기, 벨웨더 시장이 나타났습니다. 주디는 그들이 무엇을 알게 되었는지 설명했지만, 벨웨더는 이미 알고 있었습니다. 그녀가 바로 포식자들을 야만적으로 변하게 만든 범인이었습니다! 벨웨더는 먹이가 지배할 때가 되었다고 생각했습니다. 그렇게 되기 위한 유일한 방법은 다른 이들이 포식자들을 두려워하게 하는 것이었죠!

....

p.29

🔵 닉과 주디가 출구로 빠르게 달려가자, 숫양들이 보관함을 쳐서 닉의 손에서 떨어뜨렸습니다. 벨웨더는 총을 꺼내서 독이 든 탄알로 닉을 쏘았습니다!

....

p.30

🔵 닉이 네 발로 엎드렸고 주디를 향해 달려들었습니다. 그가 야만적으로 변해 버렸어요!

주디가 뒤로 물러났습니다. "그래서 그게 전부인가요. 먹이는 포식자들을 두려워하고 당신은 권력을 유지하고?"

벨웨더가 히죽거리며 웃었습니다. "공포는 *언제나* 효과가 있어. 그리고 난 주토피아에 있는 모든 포식자들에게 총을 쏴서라도 그렇게 유지할 거야."

p.31

🔵 바로 그때, 닉이 일어섰습니다. 예상과 달리 그는 야만적으로 변하지 않았어요! 그가 총에 들어 있는 꽃으로 만든 탄알을 주디의 트럭에서 가져온 블루베리로 바꿔서 벨웨더가 자백하도록 속였던 것이었습니다.

벨웨더는 걱정하지 않았습니다. "내 말과 반대되는 너희의 주장만 있을 뿐이야!"

하지만 주디는 그 고백을 녹음해 두었습니다.

ZPD가 벨웨더를 체포하자, 닉과 주디는 그녀를 향해 미소 지었습니다. "그걸 바로 사기라고 하는 거야, 얘야. 짜잔."

p.32

🔵 곧 주토피아는 정상으로 돌아왔습니다. 닉은 경찰이 되어 주디의 새로운 파트너가 되었습니다! 주디는 심지어 닉의 경찰 학교 졸업식에서 졸업 연설을 했습니다. 그녀는 새로운 경찰관들에게 그들로부터 변화가 시작된다는 점을 상기시켰습니다. 그들은 주토피아에 사는 동물들에게 어떻게 더 나은 세상을 건설할 수 있는지 보여 줄 수 있었습니다.

주디는 닉을 향해 자랑스럽게 미소 지었습니다.

그 둘 덕분에, 주토피아의 주민들은 함께 일한다면, 모두 자신들이 사는 곳을 더 좋은 곳으로 만들 수 있다는 사실을 배우게 되었습니다.

Answer

Vocabulary Quiz

1
F	Z	T	L	P	R	K	A	F	B	G	A
L	H	D	W	B	A	C	K	W	A	R	D
A	T	B	X	J	I	L	W	F	X	W	O
S	O	U	D	X	R	O	R	D	I	V	R
H	U	S	T	L	E	I	W	H	S	L	A
L	Y	T	W	F	T	A	K	M	L	C	B
B	N	L	G	K	T	M	T	H	Y	Z	L
P	R	I	O	R	I	T	Y	E	N	R	E
A	S	N	S	W	B	S	C	I	G	W	S
H	Q	G	H	F	E	L	L	O	W	A	P
X	Z	T	M	B	J	H	X	Q	H	T	E
E	S	U	S	P	I	C	I	O	U	S	K

fellow 동료의 /
suspicious 수상쩍어하는 /
flash 휙 내보이다 /
bustling 북적거리는 / **sly** 교활한 /
backward 뒤떨어진 /
priority 우선 사항 / **hustle** 사기 (행위) /
adorable 사랑스러운

2 1 mammal 2 step in 3 fool
    4 attitude 5 badge
    6 disappointed 7 sidewalk
    8 burn up 9 treat 10 hop
    11 stand up for 12 melt 13 folk

| ANSWER
They melted it down and made
"pawsicles" to sell.

Comprehension Quiz

1 3 - 4 - 2 - 1

2 1 a 2 c 3 c

3 1 true 2 false 3 true
    4 true 5 false

Vocabulary Quiz

1
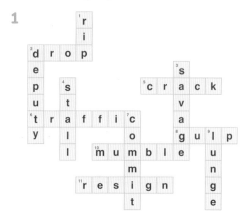

2 1 teensy 2 bruised 3 damage
    4 clue 5 confused 6 bet
    7 strike out 8 lead 9 give up
    10 deal 11 technically
    12 track 13 shred 14 otter

| ANSWER
That Judy still had time left
to solve the case

Comprehension Quiz

1 1 c 2 b

2 1 a 2 b 3 b

3 1 true 2 true 3 true
    4 false 5 false

Vocabulary Quiz

1

R	E	V	E	R	T	C	P	B	C	S	F
T	L	H	K	I	Q	H	G	M	H	B	A
J	D	N	F	Y	V	E	U	E	A	L	Z
M	O	A	O	T	F	J	A	X	O	W	R
D	V	U	O	N	A	R	R	E	S	T	T
J	E	M	T	N	X	T	D	A	C	N	K
F	R	Q	S	H	I	F	O	Z	M	J	P
A	H	F	T	J	B	L	S	N	E	A	K
F	E	Z	E	C	M	V	L	S	R	M	W
S	A	P	P	O	I	N	T	E	D	W	X
H	R	T	X	A	E	H	M	P	A	S	C
S	O	Q	I	N	S	T	I	N	C	T	V

footstep 발소리 / **appointed** 임명된 /
chaos 혼돈, 혼란 / **guard** 지키다 /
revert 되돌아가다 /
sneak 살금살금 가다 / **instinct** 본능 /
overhear 우연히 듣다 / **arrest** 체포하다

2 1 howl   2 include   3 primitive
    4 crop   5 storm off   6 impressed
    7 entrance   8 detective   9 scold
    10 prey   11 imprisoned
    12 distracted   13 row   14 present

| ANSWER
Nick was deeply hurt by Judy's
comments about predators.

Comprehension Quiz

1   4 - 2 - 1 - 3
2   1 b   2 c   3 a
3   1 false   2 true   3 true
     4 false   5 false

Vocabulary Quiz

1

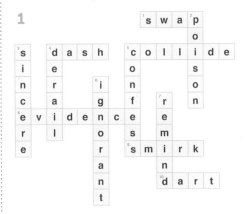

2   1 small-minded   2 in charge
    3 knock   4 trick
    5 lab   6 pellet   7 return   8 race
    9 abandoned   10 irresponsible
    11 proudly

| ANSWER
Bellwether shot him with a
blueberry.

Comprehension Quiz

1   1 b   2 b
2   1 c   2 a   3 c
3   1 false   2 true   3 true
     4 true   5 false

Character Chart   p.54

| EXAMPLE
My favorite character is Flash.
I think Flash(he) is easy-going,
sociable, and polite.

Disney
ZOOTOPIA
Read-Along

초판 발행   2022년 8월 5일

지은이   Disney Press
번역및콘텐츠제작   정소이 Julie Tofflemire
영문감수   Sherwood Choe
편집   정소이 유아름
디자인   박새롬 이순영
저작권   김보경
마케팅   김보미 정경훈

기획   김승규
펴낸이   이수영
펴낸곳   롱테일북스
출판등록   제2015-000191호
주소   04033 서울특별시 마포구 양화로 113(서교동), 3층
전자메일   helper@longtailbooks.co.kr
(학원·학교에서 본도서를 교재로 사용하길 원하시는 경우 전자메일로 문의주시면
자세한 안내를 받으실 수 있습니다.)

ISBN 979-11-91343-40-3 14740

JUDY

NICK

CHIEF BOGO

FLASH

DEPUTY MAYOR BELLWETHER

MAYOR LIONHEART

Disney
ZOOTOPIA
Read Along

Storybook

Long tail Books

ISBN 979-11-91343-40-3 14740
Longtail Books

Disney

ZOOTOPIA

Read Along

• Storybook •

Judy Hopps was excited. She had **graduate**d at the top of her class from the police **academy**. Now she was leaving her family's farm and going to the **bustling** city of Zootopia. She was going to be the city's first-ever bunny **cop**. No one believed a bunny could make a good cop, but Judy **was determined to prove** them wrong!

As Judy **made her way** to her apartment, she looked around. Zootopia was filled with animals of all shapes and sizes! She couldn't wait to begin her new life!

3

The next morning, Judy **introduce**d herself to her **fellow officer**s at the Zootopia Police **Department**. "Hey. Officer Hopps. You ready to make the world a better place?"

Soon **Chief** Bogo walked in. "We have fourteen **missing mammal case**s. Fourteen cases! And that's more than we've ever had. This is **priority** number one."

Chief Bogo **assign**ed each officer a missing mammal case. Then he came to Judy. "And finally, our first bunny, Officer Hopps. **Parking duty**."

Judy was **disappointed**. But if she had to be a **meter maid**, she'd be the best one possible!

Judy was writing parking **ticket**s when she saw a fox entering Jumbeaux's Café. **Suspicious**, she followed him.

But when she got inside, Judy saw that the fox was just trying to buy a Jumbo-pop for his son, who was dressed as an elephant. "My boy, this **goofy** little stinker, he loves all things elephant. Wants to be one when he grows up. That **adorable**? Who the heck am I to **crush** his little dreams, huh?"

When the owner **refuse**d to **serve** the fox, Judy **step**ped **in** and **flash**ed her **badge**. If the little fox wanted a Jumbo-pop, she was going to make sure he got one!

Grumbling, the shop owner **hand**ed **over** a
Jumbo-pop. But when the father fox reached for his
wallet, he realized he didn't have it.

Judy offered to pay. "Oh, no, my **treat**. It's just—
you know, it **burn**s me **up** to see **folk**s with such **backward**
attitudes toward foxes."

Outside, Judy introduced herself to the fox, whose name
was Nick. Then she turned to his son. "And you, little guy.
You want to be an elephant when you grow up? You be an
elephant, because this is Zootopia. Anyone can be anything."

Later, Judy saw Nick and his "son" on the **sidewalk**. It **turn**ed **out** Nick's son was not a child at all. He was an adult fox! The **pair** had **fool**ed Judy to get a free Jumbo-pop. Now they were **melt**ing down the Jumbo-pop and **refreezing** it into smaller "pawpsicles," which they were selling to lemmings. Judy couldn't believe it!

Judy **caught up** to Nick. "I **stood up for** you, and you lied to me!"

Nick **shrug**ged. "It's called a **hustle**, sweetheart. All right, look, everyone comes to Zootopia thinking they can be anything they want. Well, you can't. You can only be what you are."

Nick pointed to himself—"**Sly** fox"—and then Judy—"**Dumb** bunny."

That hurt Judy's feelings. "I am *not* a dumb bunny!"

"Right. And that's not wet **cement**."

Judy looked down. She had **hop**ped into some drying cement.

Nick shook his head. "You'll never be a real cop."

The next day, a pig ran up to Judy. His flower shop had just been robbed by a **weasel**!

Judy **chase**d the **bandit** all around Little Rodentia before finally catching him. But when Judy brought the thief to ZPD, Chief Bogo was angry. The chase had caused a lot of **damage**.

Judy was **confused**. "Sir, I got the bad guy. That's my job."

"Your job is putting tickets on parked cars."

Suddenly, Judy and Chief Bogo were interrupted by a very **upset** Mrs. Otterton. Her husband had been missing for ten days!

Judy knew this was her **chance**. She offered to find Mr. Otterton.

Before Chief Bogo could argue, **Deputy Mayor** Bellwether appeared. She had heard that Judy was taking the case. She was **thrilled**.

Chief Bogo had no choice. "I will give you forty-eight hours. But, you **strike out**, you **resign**."

Judy **gulp**ed. "Oh, uh . . . okay. **Deal**."

Judy's only **clue** in the case was a photo of Mr. Otterton. In it, he was eating a pawpsicle. That meant Nick knew him!

Judy went to find the sly fox. She tricked him into admitting that he had **commit**ted a **crime** and made him agree to help her.

Judy and Nick soon found out that Mr. Otterton had been seen getting into a car with the license plate 29THD03. The pair went to the DMV, where Nick's friend Flash the **sloth** worked.

Judy **approach**ed Flash. "Well, I was hoping you could **run** a plate for us."

Flash agreed. But the sloth moved so slowly that it took him all day to get Judy the answer! Nick had known talking to Flash would **stall** Judy. He was trying to get her to **give up**! But the bunny **was**n't **about to drop** the case.

Finally, Nick and Judy learned that Mr. Otterton had been driven away in the back of a limo. The duo **track**ed the limo to a **parking lot.** When they looked inside, they were shocked. The back seat was **rip**ped to **shred**s.

The two went to find the driver, a **jaguar** named Mr. Manchas. When Manchas opened his door, the pair saw that he was badly **bruised.** He told them that Mr. Otterton had **attack**ed him!

"Woah. A **teensy otter** . . . did *that*?"

Mr. Manchas explained that Mr. Otterton had been **mumbling** about "night howlers" before he went **savage**.

Suddenly, Mr. Manchas dropped to all fours. Without warning, he **lunge**d at Judy and Nick. He had gone savage, too!

Nick and Judy tried to **capture** Mr. Manchas, but he had escaped. When they explained to Chief Bogo what had happened, he **demand**ed Judy's badge.

Before Judy could agree, Nick **step**ped **forward**. "Here's the thing, Chief, you gave her the forty-eight hours, so **technically** we still have ten left to find our Mr. Otterton. And that's exactly what we're gonna do. So if you'll excuse us, we have a very big **lead** to follow and a case to **crack**."

Judy was surprised to see Nick stand up for her. She realized that there was more to the fox than she had first thought. Maybe the two weren't so different after all.

Then Nick had an idea. They could use the **traffic** cameras to see where the savage Mr. Manchas had gone.

Nick and Judy visited Deputy Mayor Bellwether. The two watched on her cameras as a group of wolves hopped out of a van and **grab**bed Mr. Manchas.

As one of the wolves howled, Judy realized something. "Night howlers. That's what Manchas was afraid of . . . wolves! The wolves are the night howlers. If they took Manchas . . ."

"I **bet** they took Otterton, too."

Nick studied the screen. It didn't take him long to **figure out** where the wolves were going: the Cliffside **Asylum**.

Judy was **impressed**. "Well look at you, **junior detective**. You know, I think you'd actually make a pretty good cop."

When the pair reached the asylum, they found the **entrance guard**ed by wolves. Judy **howl**ed. Soon all the wolves were howling, too.

With the wolves **distracted**, Judy and Nick **snuck** inside . . .
where they found **row**s of **cage**s with **imprisoned predator**s—
including Mr. Otterton!

Judy counted the cages: ". . . eleven, twelve, thirteen,
fourteen. Chief Bogo **hand**ed **out** fourteen missing mammal
files. All the missing mammals are right here."

Suddenly, Nick and Judy heard **footstep**s. The pair hid. A moment later, they heard a voice. It was the mayor. He knew all about the savage animals and was keeping it a secret!

Taking out her phone, Judy **record**ed the mayor. Then her phone began to ring. She and Nick had to get out of the asylum before they were caught!

The pair **narrowly escape**d. Back at ZPD, Judy **present**ed
her recording to Chief Bogo. Impressed, he let *her* **arrest** the
mayor.

A short time later, the newly **appointed** Mayor Bellwether
held a **press conference**. When Judy was asked to speak, she
presented the facts about the animals who had gone savage.

"All we know is that they are all members of the predator **family**. Thousands of years ago, predators **survive**d through their **aggressive** hunting **instinct**s. For whatever reason, they seem to be **revert**ing back to their **primitive** savage ways."

Nick was hurt by her words. Did she think he could turn into a savage predator?

Turning his back on Judy, Nick **storm**ed **off**.

The press conference **divide**d Zootopia. Soon it was **prey** versus predator.

Judy felt so bad about the **chaos** she had caused that she quit the ZPD and moved home. A few days later, she **overhear**d her father **scold**ing some kids for running through the flowers at the **edge** of his field.

When Judy heard her father's friend Gideon **refer** to the same flowers as night howlers, she realized something. "Night howlers aren't wolves. They're flowers."

Judy's father explained that the flowers kept the bugs away from his **crop**s, but they could also make animals **go crazy**.

Judy remembered from her case file that Mr. Otterton was a florist. "The flowers are making the predators go savage. That's it! That's what I've been missing!"

Judy jumped in her family's blueberry truck and drove back to the city. She found Nick and **apologize**d to him. "I was **ignorant** and **irresponsible** and **small-minded**. I have to fix this, but I can't do it without you."

Nick knew Judy was **sincere**. He **forgave** her.

Judy told Nick what she had learned about the flowers. Together, they followed their clues to a secret **lab** in an **abandoned** subway car. Inside, a group of **ram**s were turning night howlers into **poison pellet**s they could **shoot** at predators to make them go savage.

Judy knew what they had to do. "We need to get this **evidence** to the ZPD!"

Nick and Judy **took control of** the subway car. But the rams tried to stop them. After almost **colliding** with another train, their train **derail**ed and **caught on fire, destroy**ing the flowers. Nick held up a case with a gun and a night howler pellet inside. They still had their evidence!

The pair **race**d through the Natural History Museum on their way to ZPD. Suddenly, Mayor Bellwether appeared. Judy explained what they had learned, but Bellwether already knew. She was the one making the predators turn savage! Bellwether thought it was time for prey to be **in charge**. The only way for that to happen was to make them fear the predators!

As Nick and Judy **dash**ed for the exit, the rams **knock**ed the case out of Nick's hands. Bellwether pulled out the gun and shot Nick with the poison pellet!

Nick dropped to all fours and lunged at Judy. He had turned savage!

Judy backed up. "So that's it. Prey fears predator and you stay in power?"

Bellwether **smirk**ed. "Fear *always* works. And I'll **dart** every predator in Zootopia to keep it that way."

Just then, Nick stood up. He hadn't gone savage after all! He had **swap**ped the flower pellet in the gun with a blueberry from Judy's truck to **trick** Bellwether into **confess**ing.

Bellwether wasn't worried. "It's my word **against** yours!"

But Judy had recorded the confession.

As the ZPD arrested Bellwether, Nick and Judy smiled at her. "It's called a hustle, sweetheart. Boom."

Soon Zootopia **return**ed to normal. Nick became
a cop and Judy's new partner! Judy even gave the
commencement speech at Nick's police academy
graduation. She **remind**ed the new officers that change
started with them. They could show the animals of
Zootopia how to build a better world.

Judy smiled at Nick **proudly**.

Thanks to the two of them, the **resident**s of Zootopia
had learned that, working together, they could all make
their home a better place.

Read-Along

Zootopia, where anyone can be anything

When animals start to go missing in Zootopia, officer Judy Hopps, the city's first bunny cop, jumps at the chance to solve the mystery. Follow along as Judy and scam-artist fox Nick Wilde race to crack their case.